Literacy:
Guided Reading Rotation Programme

Book 1: Year 3

Janet Bruce

Title:	Literacy: Guided Reading Rotation Programme Book 1: Year 3
Author:	Janet Bruce
Editor:	Paula Wagemaker
Layout:	Freshfields Design Limited
Book Code:	358A
ISBN:	978-1-877498-70-1
Published:	2008
Publisher:	Essential Resources Educational Publishers Limited

United Kingdom:	*Australia:*	*New Zealand:*
Unit 8–10 Parkside	PO Box 90	PO Box 5036
Shortgate Lane	Oak Flats	Invercargill 9810
Laughton	NSW 2529	ph: 0800 087 376
BN8 6DG	ph: 1800 005 068	fax: 0800 937 825
ph: 0845 3636 147	fax: 1800 981 213	
fax: 0845 3636 148		

Website:	www.essentialresources.uk.com
Copyright:	Text © Janet Bruce, 2008 Edition and illustrations: © Essential Resources Educational Publishers Limited, 2008
About the author:	Janet Bruce has taught at all levels of the primary school. As a curriculum coordinator, her primary responsibilities were to develop the school-based English curriculum. Janet initially developed the guided reading programme that is the focus of this present resource while teaching lower primary pupils. She then adapted it when teaching other year groups. The resource has emerged from her passion for reading and inspiring younger children to develop a love of reading. The open-ended tasks that appear in this fun resource are therefore a product of her detailed knowledge of English and literacy curricula, as well as her varied classroom experience.

Photocopy notice:

Permission is given to schools and teachers who buy this book to reproduce it (and/or any extracts) by photocopying or otherwise, but only for use at their present school. Copies may not be supplied to anyone else or made or used for any other purpose.

Contents

Notes For Teachers: The Guided Reading Book Club

What is a Guided Reading Book Club?	4
Setting up a Guided Reading Book Club	5
What Are Literacy Rotation Activities?	6
The Literacy Rotation Activities	7
Using the Activity (Task) Cards	8
Book Marks	9
Curriculum Links	9
Organisation of the Guided Reading Groups and the Literacy Rotation Activities	10

For Pupils: The Book Club Meeting

Book Club Meeting Guidelines	11
Book Club Discussion Questions	12

Literacy Rotation Activity Cards

Comprehension and Detail Cards 1–20

Language and Vocabulary Cards 1–20

Artist and Illustrator Cards 1–20

Reflecting and Responding Cards 1–20

Notes For Teachers: The Guided Reading Book Club

This section, written for teachers, provides a range of discussion points and suggestions that you can use while taking a guided reading group.

What is a Guided Reading Book Club?

Guided reading is an activity where pupils gather together with the teacher to read a section of a book. Afterwards, the group discusses the book and the development of the story. The main focus of the Guided Reading Book Club is for the pupils to engage in dialogue about the text they are reading and to do this at regular intervals as the book progresses. The club provides you, the teacher, with a good opportunity to discuss features of the text and to engage your pupils at a deeper level.

Group your pupils according to needs, based on reliable classroom-based assessment procedures. The Guided Reading Book Club is an excellent method for developing higher-order thinking skills in those pupils who are already reading.

The Guided Reading Book Club requires a group of pupils to select a text from several that you offer. The text should suit the reading interests and reading ability of the group's members. Pupils must each have their own copy of the text.

When the children first receive a book, their initial discussion should focus on the cover and title to encourage the group to make predictions on content. Subsequent discussions should focus on deepening the pupils' understandings of the text and on encouraging their higher-order thinking.

Pupils benefit significantly when participating in a Guided Reading Book Club. The many strategies provided enable them to build greater meaning from the text and to increase their comprehension. This development, in turn, allows them to develop greater fluency and reading skills.

Setting up a Guided Reading Book Club

The aim of the discussion the children engage in during the Guided Reading Book Club is to encourage open, natural conversation, where personal opinions, experiences and questions are welcomed and explored. Your role is that of facilitator, not a group member or instructor.

1. Group your pupils according to their reading ability.

2. Each group should consist of four or six pupils.

3. Ask each group of pupils to sit in a circle, and then take turns to read the book aloud.

4. Make sure each pupil has their own copy of the book so they can follow along and that they also have a number of book marks (see page 9).

5. Also make sure that each group has a book that is appropriate for their reading level and a task activity card as appropriate (see following pages).

6. Have the groups meet regularly to read so they can discuss a section of the text at a time.

7. At the beginning of each section, ask the pupils to briefly discuss the section of the book they read during "independent reading" and then to take turns reading the next section of the book aloud.

8. Encourage their discussion of each section of the book by answering questions from the "Book Club Discussion Questions" list (see page 12). This list can be copied and laminated, making it a handy resource to use with any book.

9. Also encourage your pupils to clarify their understanding by asking the other members of the group questions.

10. Assess the children while listening to their individual reading and their responses to the questions. Also assess the extent and nature of their participation and their book work.

What Are Literacy Rotation Activities?

Literacy rotation activities consist of five different small group activities that run in conjunction with the teacher taking a small group of pupils who are participating in the Guided Reading Book Club.

The literacy rotation activities (given in this resource as a series of task cards) provide pupils with stimulating and fun activities that explore different facets of their book. The activities are self-sufficient in that they provide pupils with clear direction and expectations, thereby allowing the teacher to engage with the book club group without distractions. The literacy rotation activities cover important areas of the curriculum as outlined on the next page.

Teacher with a Guided Reading Book Club

Independent Reading Group	Comprehension and Detail Group (Activity cards)	Language and Vocabulary Group (Activity cards)	Artist and Illustrator Group (Activity cards)	Reflecting and Responding Group (Activity cards)

The Literacy Rotation Activities

Independent Reading

This activity requires pupils to read the next section of their book independently. Each pupil should write on their book mark any interesting or unusual words they come across as they read. When the book club meets the following week, they will discuss the section of the book read during "Independent Reading" before beginning their Guided Reading Book Club session with the teacher.

Comprehension and Detail

These activities aim to develop pupils' comprehension. The activities are varied and encourage the pupils to engage with the text to extract greater meaning.

Language and Vocabulary

These activities focus on language, grammar, understanding and applying new vocabulary. The activities encourage pupils to seek out, identify, understand and apply new and interesting words.

Artist and Illustrator

These activities explore the creative and visual aspects of the book. They also explore the emotions and pictures created in our minds when we hear particular words, phrases, and passages. The activities enable pupils to visualise the thoughts and feelings they have in relation to the text and to re-create these artistically.

Reflecting and Responding

These activities ask pupils to reflect on and respond to a particular aspect of their text to provoke a written response. These activities are particularly interesting for pupils because they enable them to respond in a personal manner.

Using the Activity (Task) Cards

The cards are designed to be photocopied, cut out and laminated. There are 20 cards in each section, which means you will have a full year's supply of task cards to use. The timetable on page 10 provides you with a clear fortnightly timetable that allows each group to rotate through all activities over the two-week period.

Each fortnight, select one card for each of the following groups:
- Comprehension and Detail
- Language and Vocabulary
- Artist and Illustrator
- Reflecting and Responding.

I keep these cards all together in an envelope at the front of the classroom, attached to the organisation board. As the diagram below shows, the board displays the names of each of the children in each group and a copy of the timetable. I also have a pocket for additional book marks that the children can take and use when needed. (For information about the book marks, see page 9.)

The activity cards are designed to be used as follows:
- One card (laminated) is handed to each group completing that activity.
- The children read the activity on the card.
- The children write all responses in their own literacy rotation exercise books.

When it is time for the Guided Reading and Literacy Rotation Activities to begin, one person from each group collects the activity card for the group. All other children collect their books and any other materials required and begin the task card. The children sit together in their groups to complete the activities.

Example of Display Board

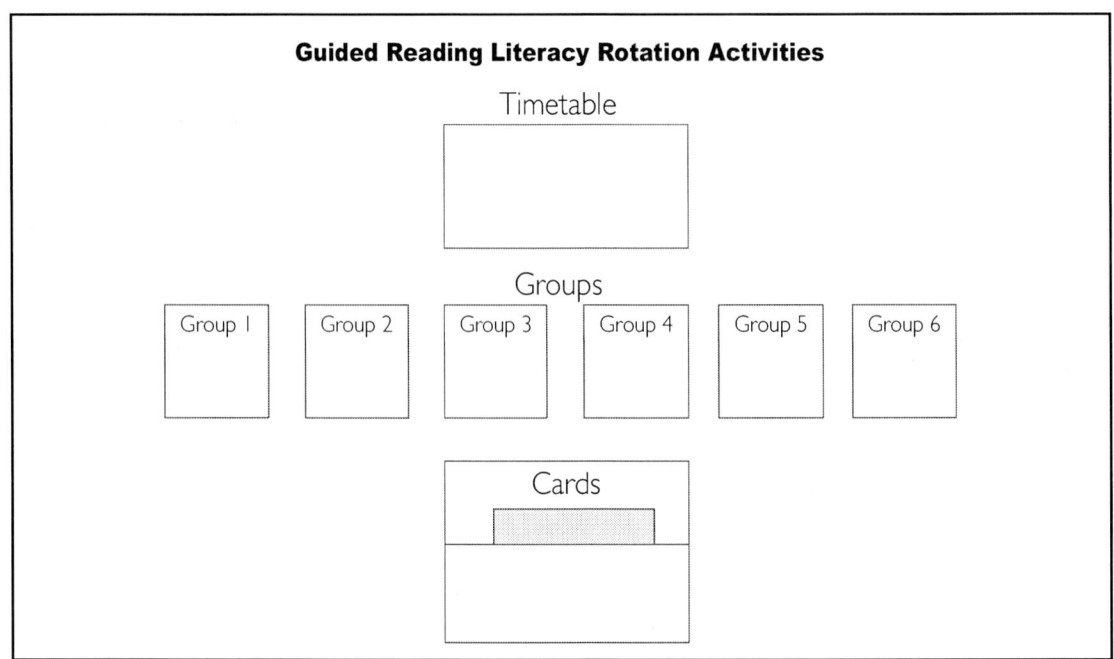

Book Marks

The children use the book marks mainly during the independent reading and guided reading sessions. As the children read the book, they should write down any unusual or unknown words on the book mark. They then use these words for some of the activities in the Language and Vocabulary section. When children identify and write down new or difficult words, they are strengthening and broadening their own vocabularies.

Name: _____

Book: _____

Author: _____

Words:

Curriculum Links

Key Stage 2 (Year 3)

Learning strand	Objective(s) *Most children learn to:*
3. Group discussion and interaction	• Use talk to organise roles and action • Actively include and respond to all members of the group
7. Understanding and interpreting texts	• Infer characters' feelings in fiction and consequences in logical explanations • Explore how different texts appeal to readers
8. Engaging with and responding to texts	• Share and compare reasons for reading preferences, extending the range of books read • Empathise with characters and debate moral dilemmas portrayed in texts • Identify features that writers use to provoke readers' reactions
9. Creating and shaping texts	• Use layout, format, graphics and illustrations for different purposes

Source: Adapted from the Primary Framework for Literacy and Maths 2006

Organisation of the Guided Reading Groups and the Literacy Rotation Activities

		Odd Week			Even Week		
		Session 1	Session 2	Session 3	Session 1	Session 2	Session 3
Group 1	1 2 3 4 5	Book Club	Comprehension and Detail	Language and Vocabulary	Independent Reading	Reflect and Respond	Artist and Illustrator
Group 2	1 2 3 4 5	Artist and Illustrator	Book Club	Comprehension and Detail	Language and Vocabulary	Independent Reading	Reflect and Respond
Group 3	1 2 3 4 5	Reflect and Respond	Artist and Illustrator	Book Club	Comprehension and Detail	Language and Vocabulary	Independent Reading
Group 4	1 2 3 4 5	Independent Reading	Reflect and Respond	Artist and Illustrator	Book Club	Comprehension and Detail	Language and Vocabulary
Group 5	1 2 3 4 5	Language and Vocabulary	Independent Reading	Reflect and Respond	Artist and Illustrator	Book Club	Comprehension and Detail
Group 6	1 2 3 4 5	Comprehension and Detail	Language and Vocabulary	Independent Reading	Reflect and Respond	Artist and Illustrator	Book Club

© Essential Resources Educational Publishers Ltd, 2008

Book Club
Meeting Guidelines

You will need your book, a pencil and your book mark.

1. Form a circle.
2. Get organised within one minute.
3. Briefly summarise what happened in the last section of the book you read independently.
4. Read the next section of the book.
5. Take turns to read small sections of the text and follow along as others read.
6. Cooperate with your group and support one another with reading.
7. Discuss the section you have just read. If you have any questions, ask your group.
8. Finally, choose a few questions to answer from the "Book Club Discussion Questions" list.

Book Club Discussion Questions

- What do you like about the way the book started?
- Where does the story take place?
- What do you think will happen next?
- How are the characters alike?
- How are the characters different?
- Does this book remind you of another book? Explain why.
- Which character is most like you? Explain why.
- What was the main event in the story?
- Find THREE good describing words the author used in the story.
- What do you think might happen next?
- What did you like or dislike about the story?
- How could the story be made more exciting?
- How did the author show characters speaking?
- What is your favourite picture?
- Did the characters do something unusual? What was it?
- How did the author finish the story?
- Open your book to the page when _____.
- Find _____.

Comprehension and Detail

Aim

The aim of the comprehension and detail activities is to develop pupils' comprehension and understanding of the text. The activities encourage pupils to engage with the text to extract a greater depth of meaning and understanding.

Comprehension and Detail

CARD 1

What Happened?

Write a few sentences to describe what happened in the book. Your sentences should describe not only the main events in the story but also the important details that occurred in the story.

Comprehension and Detail

CARD 2

Five Questions

Write FIVE questions about your book. Frame these questions so they are open-ended and require a descriptive or explanatory answer. Read your questions out to others and test their knowledge.

Comprehension and Detail

CARD 3

Main Idea Map

Create a picture map of the main events that took place in your story. Your map should include a picture of each important event that took place. Be sure to label each picture.

© Essential Resources Educational Publishers Ltd, 2008

Comprehension and Detail

CARD 4

Charming Character Traits

What kind of a person is the main character in the story? Draw a picture of the main character and write TEN good adjectives that best describe this character. Set out your page so it looks like this:

© Essential Resources Educational Publishers Ltd, 2008

Comprehension and Detail

CARD 5

Brilliant Book Title

The author of the book you have read is not very happy with the title of the book. Your job is to create a brand new and exciting title for this book. Remember to think about all of the characters and events that took place in the story while you are thinking of a new title.

Design a new illustration to go with your new title.

Comprehension and Detail

CARD 6

Book Report

You have been asked to write a book report for the other pupils at your school. Your job is to give them information about the book, such as the name of the book, a summary of the story, and your opinion about the book. The pupils will then read your book review and have information that can help them make good choices about what they read.

Comprehension and Detail

CARD 7

Character Types

There are many different types of characters in stories. Some characters might be unlike anyone you know, while other characters might remind you of someone you know. Choose ONE character from the story and give reasons why this character does or does not remind you of someone you know.

© Essential Resources Educational Publishers Ltd, 2008

Comprehension and Detail

CARD 8

Character Choices

One of the characters in your story would like help deciding what to do during the holidays. Your job is to come up with a list of fun and interesting activities for your character.

© Essential Resources Educational Publishers Ltd, 2008

Comprehension and Detail

CARD 9

Splendid Speech

Give THREE reasons why you did or did not enjoy the story. Present these ideas to your group in an oral presentation.

Comprehension and Detail

CARD 10

Author Anecdote

Pretend that you are the author of the book. Come up with THREE things you liked about the book and THREE things you could change to create a better story. Begin your statements with:

- I really liked …
- If I was the author, I would change …

Comprehension and Detail

CARD 11

Strong Story

Think about the main events that took place in the story. Choose THIRTY strong *adjectives* (describing words) and *nouns* (naming words) that outline the entire story. Choose your words carefully and read them out like a descriptive list. Your list should describe the most important parts of the story.

© Essential Resources Educational Publishers Ltd, 2008

Comprehension and Detail

CARD 12

Finding Fun

Search through your story to find FIVE unusual or interesting words. Share these words with your group and write down their meaning. Use ONE of these words in a sentence.

© Essential Resources Educational Publishers Ltd, 2008

Comprehension and Detail

CARD 13

Free Future

Describe what you think happened to the main character of the book after the book ended. Write down your ideas, then share them with your group.

Comprehension and Detail

CARD 14

Short Sequence

Write down ONE sentence that explains what happened in the beginning of the story. Then write ONE sentence that describes what happened in the middle of the story. Finally, write ONE sentence that describes what happened at the end of the story.

Comprehension and Detail

CARD 15

Speaking Sincerely

Choose FIVE *nouns* (words that name people, places or things) from your book. Use these five nouns to create a silly sentence. Read your sentence to your group.

© Essential Resources Educational Publishers Ltd, 2008

Comprehension and Detail

CARD 16

Quick Questions

Write TEN quick questions about the book you have read. The questions you write down need to have a yes or no answer so that they can be answered in no more than one minute. Give your questions to a partner in your group and time his or her answers. Now have a go at answering your partner's questions.

© Essential Resources Educational Publishers Ltd, 2008

Comprehension and Detail

CARD 17

Mr Fact

Mr Fact is looking for clues from the story you are reading. He would like your help to solve the case. Choose ONE character from the story. Create a character fact file by describing the character. *Example:*

Name: Little Red Riding Hood

Description: Young girl, approximately eight to nine years old.

Clothing: Red cape, red dress, white socks and black shoes.

Location: Last seen at Grandma's house in the woods.

© Essential Resources Educational Publishers Ltd, 2008

Comprehension and Detail

CARD 18

Question Time

If you could ask one of the characters from the story a question, which character would you choose and what would you ask this character? Write the name of the character down as a heading and write the question you would like to ask him or her. What do you think this character would say in reply?

© Essential Resources Educational Publishers Ltd, 2008

Comprehension and Detail

CARD 19

How Honest

What did you think about the story? Give the story a rating out of 10. Write TWO things you enjoyed about the story and TWO things that could be improved.

Comprehension and Detail

CARD 20

Short Summary

Summarise the story in THREE sentences. When you have done that, write THREE sentences describing what happened…

- In the beginning of the story
- During the middle of the story
- At the end of the story.

Language and Vocabulary

Aim

These activities focus on the language, grammar and vocabulary within the text. The activities encourage pupils to seek out, identify, understand and apply new and interesting words.

Language and Vocabulary

CARD 1

Word Book Mark

Create a book mark. Use your book mark to write down new and interesting words you find as you are reading. The words you write on your book mark may be words you have not seen before, or they might be words you would like to know the meaning of.

© Essential Resources Educational Publishers Ltd, 2008

Language and Vocabulary

CARD 2

Literary List

Make a list of all the interesting words from your story book that you would like to use in your own writing. Choose THREE of these words and use them in a sentence.

© Essential Resources Educational Publishers Ltd, 2008

Language and Vocabulary

CARD 3

Interesting Word Count

Choose THREE words that are used frequently throughout your story. Write these three words down and scan each page to count the number of times they are written in your story. Ask a partner to check your answers.

Example:

- I found the word *scary* THREE times in my story.

Language and Vocabulary

CARD 4

Listen and Guess

You will need to complete this activity in pairs. Take turns to read a page of your book to each other. As you read, pause occasionally and ask your partner to guess the word which belongs in that place. After the guess, the reader reads on to check the answer and to finish reading the page.

Language and Vocabulary

CARD 5

Punctuation Power

Look closely at the different kinds of punctuation in your story. Find as many different punctuation marks as you can. Record how many full stops (.), commas (,), exclamation marks (!), and speech marks (" ") you can see. Compare your results with those of other people in your group.

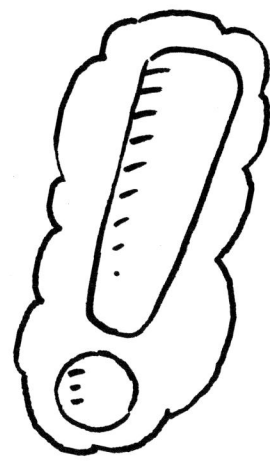

© Essential Resources Educational Publishers Ltd, 2008

Language and Vocabulary

CARD 6

Describe and Draw

You will need to complete this activity in pairs. Choose a character from the story. Describe this character to your partner. Ask your partner to draw a picture based on your description. How accurate is his or her picture? Now swap over.

© Essential Resources Educational Publishers Ltd, 2008

Language and Vocabulary

CARD 7

Read and Record

Practise reading your story on your own out loud. Try to read slowly with character voices and expression. When you are confident, record your story for others to listen to.

© Essential Resources Educational Publishers Ltd, 2008

Language and Vocabulary

CARD 8

Vibrant Verbs

A *verb* is a word that is used to describe how an action is taking place. Examples of verbs are fell, run, went, jump, sang. Find as many examples of verbs from your story as you can. List them in your book.

© Essential Resources Educational Publishers Ltd, 2008

Language and Vocabulary

CARD 9

Sounding Syllables

Words can be broken down into sections called *syllables*. It can be helpful to "feel" the syllables of a word by clapping them out.

- One-syllable words have one clap, such as **cat**, **said**, **chase**.
- Two-syllable words have two claps, such as **cov/er**, **plan/ning**.
- Three-syllable words have three claps, such as **de/liv/er**, **dis/ap/point**.

Write lists of all the one-, two- and three-syllable words you can locate in your story. Head your lists like this:

One-Syllable Words   **Two-Syllable Words**   **Three-Syllable Words**

© Essential Resources Educational Publishers Ltd, 2008

Language and Vocabulary

CARD 10

Noun Knowledge

A *noun* is a word or a group of words that refer to a person, place or thing. Examples relate to **people (children)**, **places (city)**, **things (car)**. Find as many examples of nouns from your story as you can.

List these in your book.

© Essential Resources Educational Publishers Ltd, 2008

Language and Vocabulary

CARD 11

Who Said ...

Look through your story and find other words the author has used instead of "said" (examples might be "**exclaimed**", "**shouted**", "**replied**"). Write these in your book and use them in your own writing.

© Essential Resources Educational Publishers Ltd, 2008

Language and Vocabulary

CARD 12

Contractions

Contractions are words that combine two words and leave out one or more letters. An apostrophe is left in the place where the letters are omitted. *Examples:*

- can't = can not
- didn't = did not
- haven't = have not.
- shouldn't = should not

Locate as many contractions from your story as you can. Write these in your book. Also write down the two words that make up the contraction.

© Essential Resources Educational Publishers Ltd, 2008

Language and Vocabulary

CARD 13

Anagram Puzzle

Anagrams are words that are made from the same letters as the original word. An example is **bat** to **tab**. Rearrange the letters of as many words from your book as you can to make a different word. Write these in your book.

© Essential Resources Educational Publishers Ltd, 2008

Language and Vocabulary

CARD 14

Rebus Words

A *rebus* word uses a combination of letters and pictures to represent a word. An example is **h +** *a picture of an ear* = **hear**. Look through your book and find some words that you can turn into rebus words. Remember each word must contain some letters and a picture.

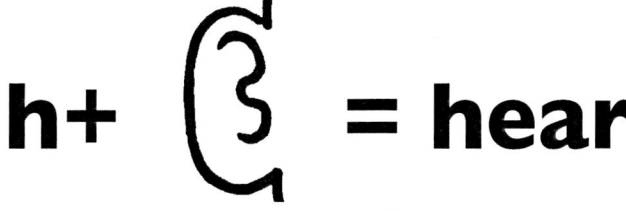

© Essential Resources Educational Publishers Ltd, 2008

Language and Vocabulary

CARD 15

Dropping Off

Sometimes we can drop a letter from a word to create a different word with a different meaning. An example is **cape = ape** or **cap**. Find as many different words from your book as you can that can be changed into another word by dropping off a letter. Write the word and the new word in your book. How many did you find?

© Essential Resources Educational Publishers Ltd, 2008

Language and Vocabulary

CARD 16

Word Sense

Create a list of *nouns* from your book. Nouns are names of people, places or things. When you have written your list, sort the nouns into two different groups. You will need to decide how you are going to sort out and classify your nouns. *Example:*

Living Things	Non-Living Things
Cat	Shoe
Plant	Spoon
Mum	Ball

© Essential Resources Educational Publishers Ltd, 2008

Language and Vocabulary

CARD 17

Feeling Feelings

Look through the story and write down all of the words that show how someone feels. Compare lists with your group when you have finished.

Language and Vocabulary

CARD 18

Perfect Pyramids

Choose a vowel (a, e, i, o, u). Write the vowel at the top of your page. Find a two-letter word containing this vowel on the second line, a three-letter word containing the vowel on the third, and so on. *Example:*

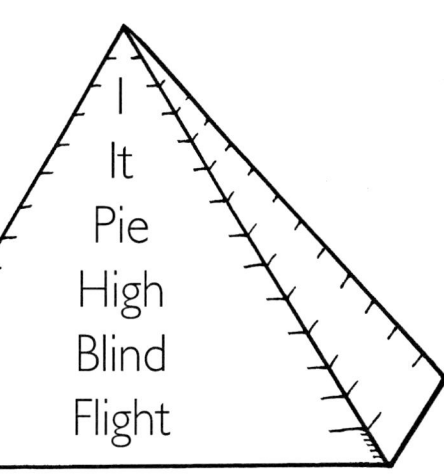

Language and Vocabulary

CARD 19

Word Categories

Scan through your story and locate all of the three- and five-letter words. Write these words as a list underneath each heading. *Example:*

Words with **Three** Letters	Words with **Five** Letters
the	drive
day	brown
sun	house

Language and Vocabulary

CARD 20

Word Dominoes

You will need each member of your group to play this game. Start by choosing a word from the story and writing this on a piece of paper. Take turns to add a word to the original word. The new word should start with the last letter of the previous word. *Example:*

Chicken / needle / egg / giant / troll / log / great / troop / pool / ladle / easy / yesterday ...

Artist and Illustrator

Aim

These activities explore creativity and visualisation. They investigate the emotions and images that are created in our minds when we hear particular words, phrases and passages. The activities enable pupils to visualise their thoughts and feelings associated with the text and to re-create these visually.

Artist and Illustrator

CARD 1

Play Dough Personality

Choose a character from your story and make him or her out of play dough. Add as much detail as you can to create a close likeness to the character.

© Essential Resources Educational Publishers Ltd, 2008

Artist and Illustrator

CARD 2

Computer Character

Create a picture of your favourite part or scene from your story. Create your picture using the computer.

© Essential Resources Educational Publishers Ltd, 2008

Artist and Illustrator

CARD 3

Finger Puppet Pal

Create a finger puppet of one of the characters from the story. Hold up your finger puppet and describe the character to your group.

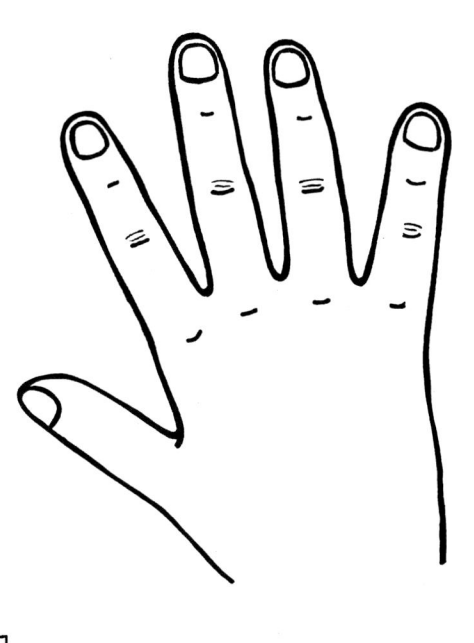

© Essential Resources Educational Publishers Ltd, 2008

Artist and Illustrator

CARD 4

Watercolour Creation

Close your eyes and think about the story you have read. What picture do you see in your mind? Paint this picture using watercolours. Share your painting with other people in your group and describe the picture.

© Essential Resources Educational Publishers Ltd, 2008

Artist and Illustrator

CARD 5

Recycled Response

Use recycled materials to create a character or object from the story. When you have finished constructing your character or object, show and describe your creation to your group.

© Essential Resources Educational Publishers Ltd, 2008

Artist and Illustrator

CARD 6

Cover Design

The author of the book would like a new front cover for it. Think about the story and design an eye-catching cover that includes some of the characters. Be sure to write the name of the story and the author's name in large, clear writing.

© Essential Resources Educational Publishers Ltd, 2008

Artist and Illustrator

CARD 7

Construction Scene

Use construction paper to create a scene from the story. Instead of cutting the paper, try tearing shapes with your fingers. Glue your pieces of torn paper onto a piece of plain paper. When your scene is complete, share it with your group and describe your scene.

© Essential Resources Educational Publishers Ltd, 2008

Artist and Illustrator

CARD 8

Draw and Find

You will need a partner for this activity. Look through the pictures in the story and choose ONE page to draw. Once you have finished your picture, show it to your partner and ask him or her to find the matching page in the story.

© Essential Resources Educational Publishers Ltd, 2008

Artist and Illustrator

CARD 9

Poster Ad

You have been asked to create a poster to advertise your book. Come up with an eye-catching design that illustrates the storyline. Make sure you write the name of the book clearly. Write a sentence stating why people should read this book. Remember that words and pictures are equally important in sending a message.

Artist and Illustrator

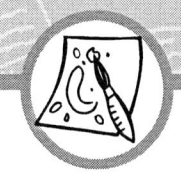

CARD 10

Pretty Portrait

A portrait is a picture of somebody's face. Portraits usually are drawn from the top of the shoulders up to the top of the head. Choose your favourite character and draw a detailed portrait of this character. When you have finished, write the name of the character and a few sentences describing him or her.

Artist and Illustrator

CARD 11

Felt Person

Use felt to create a felt character from your story. Each person in your group should create a different character so you can use them to retell the story.

© Essential Resources Educational Publishers Ltd, 2008

Artist and Illustrator

CARD 12

Incredible Illustration

Create an illustration of your favourite part of the story. Write a few sentences explaining what happened in this part of the story. Show your group what is happening in your picture.

© Essential Resources Educational Publishers Ltd, 2008

Artist and Illustrator

CARD 13

Character Clothing

Choose a character from the story. Think about what this character would like to wear. Design an outfit for this character. Label each item you design. Share your design with your group.

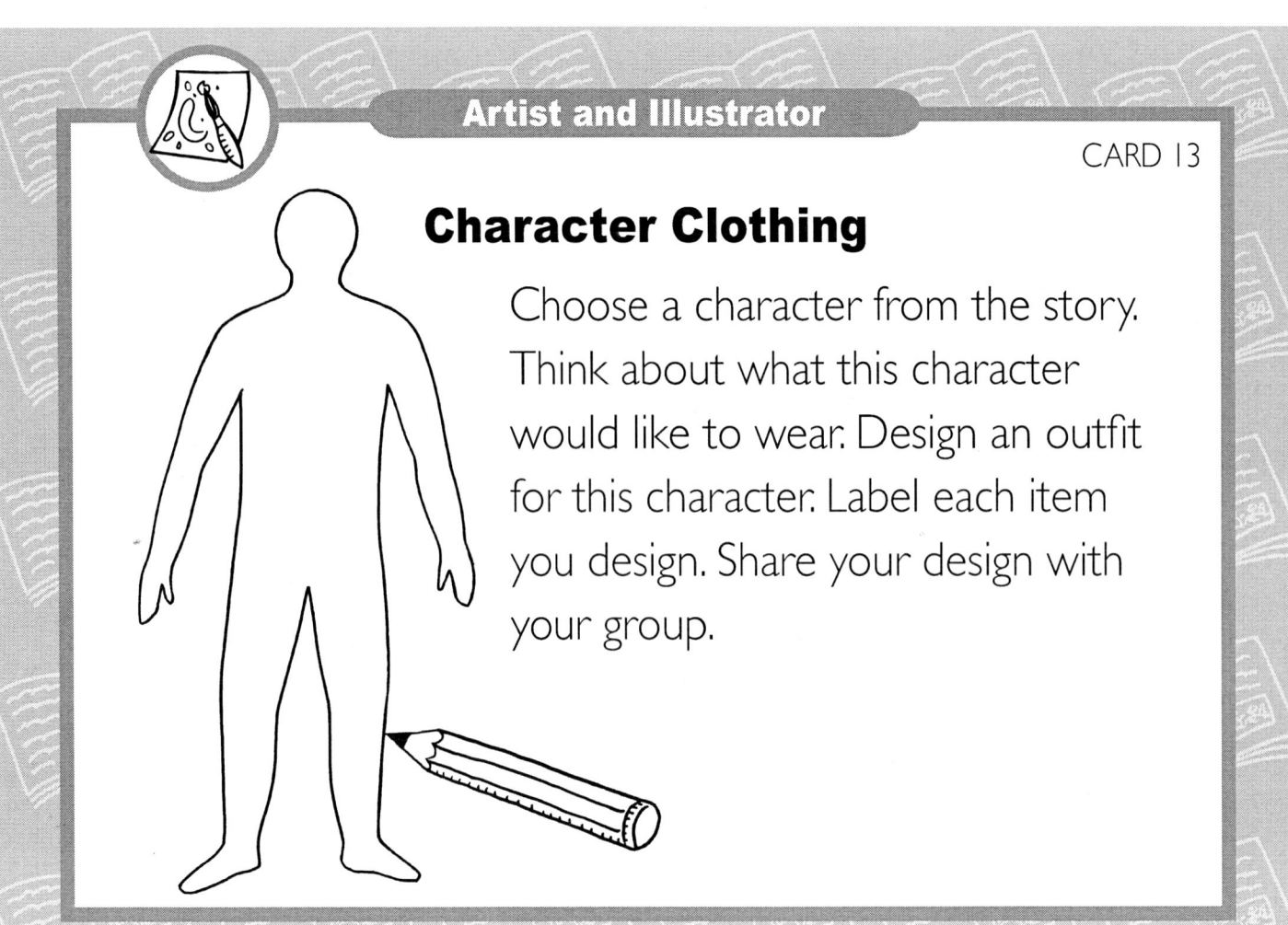

Artist and Illustrator

CARD 14

Wanted Dead Or Alive!

One of the characters from your story is wanted by the police. Create a wanted poster for a character in your story.
Be sure to draw a portrait of the character and to write his or her name. Briefly describe this person as well.

Artist and Illustrator

CARD 15

Scene Builder

You will need to work together as a team to complete this activity. Choose a scene from the story and construct the same scene using recycled materials. Look carefully at all of the things on the page and recreate these individual items. Be careful to place the items according to their location on the page.

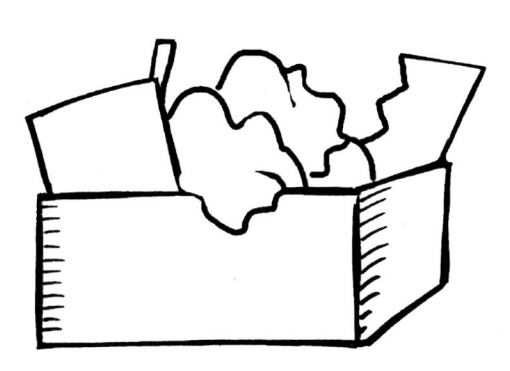

© Essential Resources Educational Publishers Ltd, 2008

Artist and Illustrator

CARD 16

Mobile Mania

Create a mobile of all the things that have a connection with the story. Draw the items on card, colour them in, cut them out and attach them to a coat-hanger with string.

© Essential Resources Educational Publishers Ltd, 2008

Artist and Illustrator

CARD 17

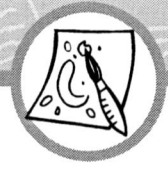

Repeated Shape Pattern

Cut out a cardboard shape of an object from the story. Using art paper, trace around this shape several times to create a repeated shape pattern. Colour the shapes using a solid colour. Display your pattern.

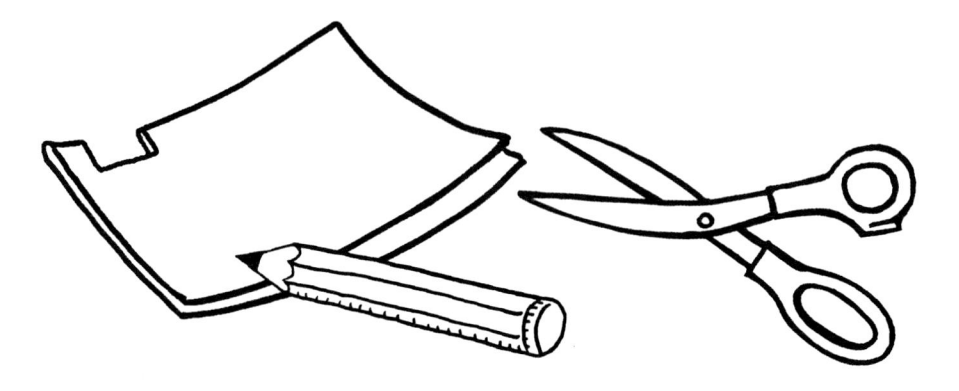

Artist and Illustrator

CARD 18

Fingerprint Characters

You will need an ink pad, paper and some coloured pencils for this activity. Press your finger on to the ink pad and then place your finger on the paper to form the head and body of the character. Use the coloured pencils to turn your fingerprint into a character from your story.

Artist and Illustrator

CARD 19

Feeling Art

Feelings can be expressed through art. Choose **two** of your favourite coloured crayons. Think about the story and let your body move the colours around the page to create a piece of art that reflects your feelings about the story. What sort of feeling is linked with a smooth flowing line? What sort of feeling is linked with a sharp, jagged line?

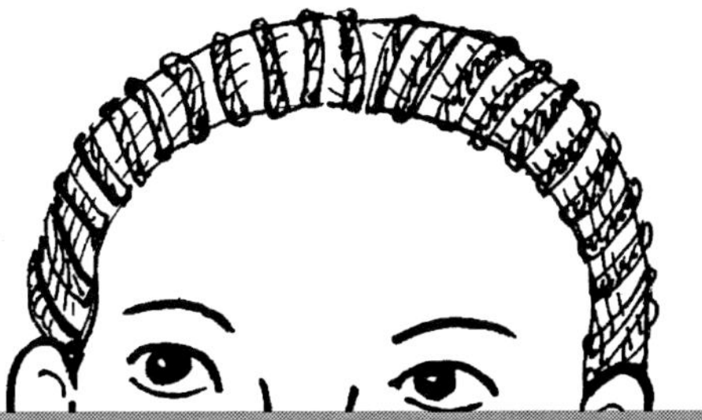

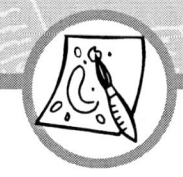

Artist and Illustrator

CARD 20

Facial Expressions

Draw your facial expression to show how you felt during the beginning, middle and end of the story. You will need to draw three separate facial expressions. Label each one with the section of the story it corresponds with:

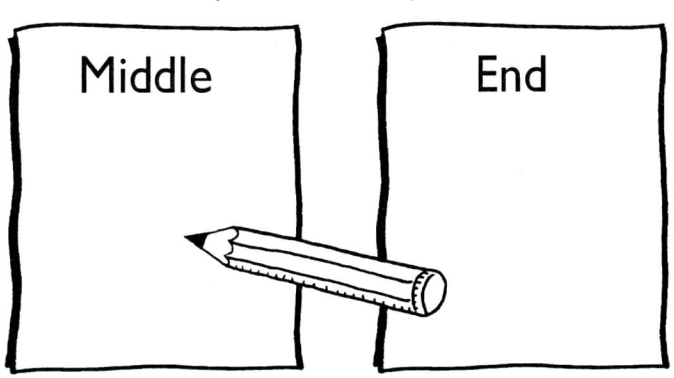

Beginning	Middle	End

Reflecting and Responding

Aim

These activities require pupils to reflect on and respond to a particular aspect of the text. They require pupils to give a thoughtful, reflective response to the text. The activities enable pupils to respond in a personal manner to the text.

Reflecting and Responding

CARD 1

Quick Question

Come up with a tricky question about the book you are reading. Be sure that you know the answer to the question yourself. Ask the people in your group to answer the question.

© Essential Resources Educational Publishers Ltd, 2008

Reflecting and Responding

CARD 2

Spot the Difference

Draw FIVE pictures of items and characters from your story. Include ONE picture that was *not* mentioned in the story. Label each picture. Show your pictures to another person in the group. Ask him or her to identify the picture that does not belong.

© Essential Resources Educational Publishers Ltd, 2008

Reflecting and Responding

CARD 3

Rhyme Time

Try to find words from your story that rhyme. If you cannot locate any rhyming words, choose some words from your story and think of a matching rhyming word for each one.

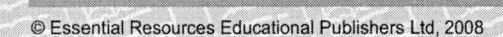

Reflecting and Responding

CARD 4

Book Look

You will need to complete this activity in pairs. Read your book together aloud, stopping at the end of each double page. Before you turn to the next page, take it in turns to guess what is going to happen next. Then turn the page and check your guess.

Reflecting and Responding

CARD 5

Wonderful Writer

Create a different ending for the story you are reading. When you have finished writing the different ending, read it out to your group.

© Essential Resources Educational Publishers Ltd, 2008

Reflecting and Responding

CARD 6

I Spy

You will need to complete this activity in pairs. Open your story at the beginning of the book. Look at the pictures this time. Take it in turns to play "I Spy" with your partner. You will need to choose an item from the pictures in the book and to know the letter of the alphabet its name begins with. Start by saying, "I spy with my little eye something beginning with …"

© Essential Resources Educational Publishers Ltd, 2008

Reflecting and Responding

CARD 7

Curly Chatter

Curl up in a comfortable place and read your story alone. When you have finished reading the story, think about what you thought of the story. Gather your thoughts and share these with another person in your group.

Reflecting and Responding

CARD 8

Interesting Information

Choose your favourite part of the story you are reading. In your exercise book, describe what happened. Explain why you liked this part.

Reflecting and Responding

CARD 9

Who Am I?

You will need to complete this activity in pairs. Play "Who am I?" based on the characters from your story. You will need to write THREE good clues about this character. Your partner will try to guess the name of the character after listening to your clues. You can start your clues by writing:

- This character is …
- This character has …
- This character …

What is the name of this character?

© Essential Resources Educational Publishers Ltd, 2008

Reflecting and Responding

CARD 10

Role Play Read

Choose an event from the book you are reading. Create ONE prop to use and then act out your chosen event to your group.

© Essential Resources Educational Publishers Ltd, 2008

Reflecting and Responding

CARD 11

Personal Point of View

Think about the story you are reading. Did anything happen in the story that you have experienced before? What happened to you?
Draw a picture of this event and describe what happened.

© Essential Resources Educational Publishers Ltd, 2008

Reflecting and Responding

CARD 12

I Would Like To Know . . .

Think about the story you are reading. Come up with a question about the book and then try to answer it. Your question should be about something you would like to know more about.

© Essential Resources Educational Publishers Ltd, 2008

Reflecting and Responding

CARD 13

Different Ending

Write a different ending for the story you are reading. Design a new picture to match your new ending.

Reflecting and Responding

CARD 14

Story Match

What sort of person would enjoy reading this book? Think about the story and the sort of person who would enjoy it.

Write a description of this person.

Reflecting and Responding

CARD 15

Full-on Feelings

How did the story make you feel? In your exercise book, describe your feelings towards the story. Try to use lots of descriptive words that truly express the way you feel about this story.

Reflecting and Responding

CARD 16

Newsletter Review

Write a review of the book for your school newsletter. Write a few sentences describing your opinion and feelings about the story. Your review should describe different parts of the book and how they made you feel.

Reflecting and Responding

CARD 17

White Hat

What are the *real events* within the story? Draw a picture of a white hat and write the real events within the hat.

Reflecting and Responding

CARD 18

Red Hat

What *feelings* did the characters in the story experience? Draw a picture of a red hat and write the feelings within the hat.

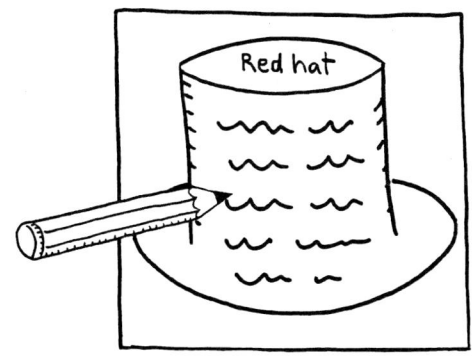

Reflecting and Responding

CARD 19

Green Hat

What are the *imaginative events* within the story? Draw a picture of a green hat and write these events within the hat.

Reflecting and Responding

CARD 20

Black Hat and Yellow Hat

What are the *bad points* and the *good points* about the story? Draw a picture of a black hat and a yellow hat. Write the bad points within the black hat and the good points within the yellow hat.